CW01004558

Picture credits:
Pictures sourced from Shutterstock Image Library.

Published By: North Parade Publishing Ltd.
4 North Parade, Bath, England.

CONTENTS

PLANETS: INTRODUCTION

A planet is any celestial body that revolves around a star. Planets and their stars are formed from massive clouds of dust and gas. Usually planets are big and massive enough to be spherical in shape, and also to have no objects of a similar size in and around their orbit.

The Greek philosopher, Ptolemy, considered both the Sun and the Moon as planets that revolved around the Earth

Understanding Planets: Over the Years

Since ancient times, it has been important to us to understand and make sense of objects in the sky. Our ancestors realised the complexity of the universe based on the numerous bodies that could be observed.

Planets weren't always known or recognised the way they are now. The ancient Greeks considered the Sun and the Moon to be planets too. In the second century CE, Greek philosopher Ptolemy listed seven planets: Moon, Mercury, Venus, Sun, Mars, Jupiter and Saturn. Earth was not considered a planet – it was simply assumed to be a celestial body around which all other objects orbited.

A land-based telescope used for studying planets

The invention of the telescope and other advancements in the field of astronomy that followed soon afterwards, led to a good understanding of the physical appearance, nature, composition and satellites (also called moons) of the different planets.

The Solar System

The Solar System is an arrangement of eight planets, along with their moons, revolving around the star (Sun) in its centre. There are millions of other objects too. These include dwarf planets, asteroids and comets. Our Solar System is a part of a much larger system – a galaxy called the 'Milky Way'. Billions of such solar systems exist in the Milky Way alone.

Beyond the planets is a region filled with billions of icy bodies and a few dwarf planets. This region is called the Kuiper Belt. Beyond that is the Oort Cloud, which is thought to be a spherical shell surrounding the Solar System, but it has not been visualised so far and merely predicted through calculations. Many comets that pass by are thought to have originated from this region.

The eight planets of our Solar System

Mercury: Mercury has been known since ancient times, and is visible to the naked eye. This small planet is a little bigger than our Moon and has no atmosphere. As a result it is covered in numerous craters caused by meteorites striking its surface. Mercury exhibits extreme temperature differences – the side facing the Sun reaches a scorching 850 degrees Fahrenheit (450 °C), the other side has temperatures approaching a hundred degrees below zero (-70 °C).

Venus: Venus is an intolerably hot planet with toxic gases and extreme pressures on the surface that would destroy life in seconds. The scorching heat of the planet is due to the greenhouse gases that trap heat and radiation. Venus has been known to people since ancient times and was mistaken to be two different stars that appeared in the morning and the evening.

Earth: Two-thirds of the 'blue planet' is covered with liquid water. Earth has gases like nitrogen and oxygen in the atmosphere that support life.

Mars: The red planet has been known since ancient times and has a distinctive red colour when observed in the night sky. It is a cold and dusty place with features like mountains and canyons. Scientists believe that Mars might have once been a wet and warm planet.

Jupiter: After the Sun, Jupiter is the most massive body in the Solar System. This gigantic planet is made up of two gases, hydrogen and helium. Jupiter has dozens of moons orbiting it and it is another object in the night sky that has been distinctly visible since ancient times.

Saturn: Saturn is the farthest planet that can be viewed without a telescope. The most characteristic feature of Saturn is its dramatic rings. Close observation and photographs revealed many fascinating features on its surface as well as plenty of moons that are considered to be complex worlds in themselves.

Uranus: Uranus was discovered by accident when an amateur astronomer was looking for double stars. This cold and windy planet is shrouded by clouds of methane making it nearly impossible to study its surface features.

Neptune: The eighth planet, Neptune, is not visible to the unaided eye or amateur telescopes, and was not discovered until mathematical calculations revealed its presence. The planet is similar to Uranus in many characteristics. A white, irregular storm cloud has been observed on its surface, zipping by at regular intervals, and nicknamed 'the scooter'.

FORMATION OF PLANETS

The Solar System is believed to have formed about 4.6 billion years ago. The biggest and most prominent member is the Sun followed by eight planets. Aside from these larger members, there are billions of other large to very small objects also present.

The Sun is Born

Our Solar System was created from a dense cloud of gas and dust, caused by the previous explosion of one or more stars. It has been predicted that at some point, the cloud collapsed after experiencing a 'shockwave' caused by an exploding star nearby.

At that time, the Solar System was a crowded messy place full of gas and debris floating everywhere. Scientists believe that the Sun, planets and all the other objects in the Solar System were formed from tiny particles smaller than the width of hair.

When the dust cloud began to collapse, it formed what is referred to as a 'solar nebula'. A solar nebula is a spinning disc of material, with a lot of material accumulating in the centre. As more and more material got pulled in, the sun began to form, simultaneously releasing a lot of energy. The Sun took up more than 99 percent of all available material.

Swirling cloud of dust and debris before the Solar System formed

Formation of Planets

Even as the Sun formed, unused matter and gases revolved around it in the form of a proto-planetary disc. The inner part of the disc is mostly rocky material as the developing Sun took up most of the gases for its own formation. Over time the matter in this disc began to clump together. The process of clumping is called accretion. These clumps collided with one another, forming even bigger clumps. The more they grew the more spherical and well-defined they became. These spherical objects became the planets, dwarf planets and their satellites.

As the Sun formed, the solar wind generated by it pushed away the remaining lighter elements such as the gases hydrogen and helium. These gases drifted far away from the Sun and formed into massive-sized planets that we know today as the gas and ice giants.

Fact File

Did you know that all the planets in the Solar System move around the Sun in the same direction that the Sun rotates?

Planets formed from the proto-planetary disc through the 'accretion' of matter

The remaining matter and debris that did not form into planets formed large, irregular objects. Many of these objects are found in an asteroid belt between Mars and Jupiter and also beyond Neptune. Some smaller objects became meteoroids, comets and asteroids.

The planets of the Solar System formed depending upon the type of matter available. The four planets closest to the Sun accumulated solid rocky material to form planets with solid surfaces. The terrestrial planets are small, rocky and have few or no moons. The planets beyond captured lighter elements like hydrogen and helium and acquired massive sizes. They are the gas giants and ice giants that lie beyond the asteroid belt. These four planets have multiple moons and have a small core surrounded by gases or ice.

STUDY OF PLANETS

For thousands of years, people have been studying the objects in the sky in an attempt to understand them. The twentieth and twenty-first centuries have been remarkable in the amount of research and findings made in the hope of better understanding of our Solar System and the universe.

Earth is not flat

Centuries ago, people from different civilizations believed that the Earth was flat. People eventually began to consider the idea of a round Earth as a better understanding of the planets developed.

Notably, the Greek philosopher and mathematician, Pythagoras at around 500 BC proposed that the Earth was spherical. Much later, in 350 BC, Aristotle used physical theory as well as evidence to prove that the Earth was a sphere. He pointed out there were constellations visible in Egypt and Cyprus that could not be seen in the northern regions. He concluded that this could only be explained by the Earth being curved.

Earth was thought to be flat in ancient times

Soon afterwards a Greek mathematician, Eratosthenes, determined the actual circumference of the Earth. In Greece as well as in other places, many different views about the shape and nature of the Earth were held. But more and more people began to accept that the Earth was spherical in shape. Much later, aircraft capable of high altitude flights and then spacecraft provided photographic proof of the Earth's shape and ended all speculations and doubts.

Greek philosopher Pythagoras stated that the Earth was a sphere

Sun is in the Centre

Nicolas Copernicus proposed the Heliocentric theory

With the deduction of Earth's shape, there was still another problem – the ancient philosophers believed that the Sun, Moon and the stars revolved around the Earth in circular orbits and that the Earth was the centre of the Universe. From the point of view of people on Earth, it does seem as if the Sun and other heavenly bodies move around the Earth. For an observer on Earth, it is difficult to perceive motion and hence the Earth was thought to be stationary.

It was only in the sixteenth century that this view was challenged by the Polish astronomer Nicolaus Copernicus. He proposed that it was the Sun which was the centre of the universe while the Earth and other planets revolved around it. This was referred to as the heliocentric (Helios – sun) theory. He had first formulated the theory as early as 1510, but his work was only published in 1543, the year he died.

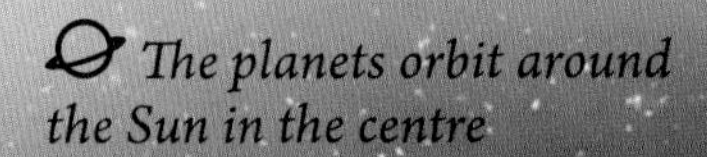

The planets orbit around the Sun in the centre

Planetary Motion

Tycho Brahe, a Danish astronomer, spent his lifetime recording planetary motion more accurately than had ever been done before. He was granted money by the King of Denmark to set up his observatory on an island to work on his project. There, Tycho Brahe built instruments and used clocks and timekeepers. He made accurate calculations long before telescopes were even invented. Johannes Kepler used these calculations to predict that the planets orbited the Sun in elliptical, not circular, orbits.

Tycho Brahe accurately predicted planetary motion even before telescopes were invented

Galileo demonstrates the use of his invention, the telescope

Invention of Telescope

Galileo Galilee invented many mechanical devices in his lifetime, but the most famous among all his inventions was the telescope. Galileo constructed his first telescope in 1609 which could magnify an object up to twenty times. The invention of the telescope was a major milestone in the observation of planets. Galileo Galilee was also able to prove Copernicus's heliocentric theory. His contributions played an important role in discovering the other planets in the Solar System and understanding the laws of physics that govern them.

Ever since the telescope was invented, the following years saw a surge in astronomical findings and understanding. Bigger and more complex telescopes were built and used to study the wonders of the sky. In the nineteenth century, the invention of a spectroscope paved the way for identifying even the composition of the planets.

Better and Advanced Telescopes

There are limitations to the optical telescopes of the kind Galileo used because they depend on lens quality and visible light. These telescopes are affected by local weather conditions and the atmosphere itself. Additionally, they are suitable for use only at nighttime as most stars and planets are not visible in the brightness of sunlight.

Recent advancements in telescopes have made it possible to provide more information and overcome some of the early limitations. These are:

- X-ray Telescopes
- Radio wave Telescopes
- Gamma Ray Telescopes
- High energy particle Telescopes

Fact File

The X-ray telescope fitted to NASA's Chandra X-ray Observatory operates at a location one-third the distance to moon.

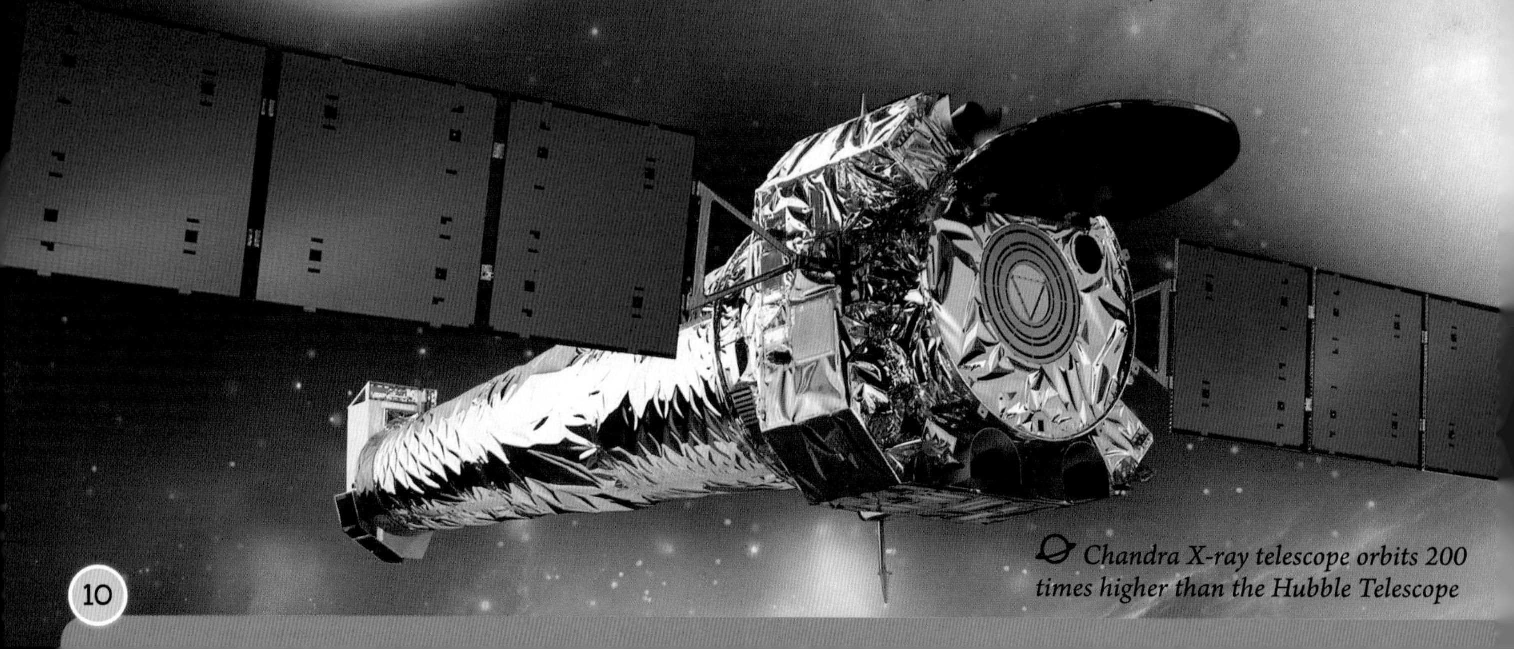

Chandra X-ray telescope orbits 200 times higher than the Hubble Telescope

Hubble Telescope

When you look up at the night sky, you're likely to see the light from the stars twinkling. Even though stars don't really twinkle, they appear to shimmer because our atmosphere bends or distorts the normally steady light from the star. Therefore, it makes sense that an object viewed through any land-based telescope, no matter how big or complex, will also be similarly distorted by the Earth's atmosphere.

Scientists looked for a way to view the universe through a telescope that was not hindered by these distortions. The European Space Agency (ESA) and National Aeronautics and Space Administration (NASA) worked together on the design and construction of a telescope that could orbit the Earth above the atmosphere.

The Hubble Telescope orbits the Earth every 96 minutes at a height of 570 kilometres. The Hubble Telescope is not hindered by the atmosphere and hence can provide incredibly detailed and clear pictures of the planets and other celestial bodies and objects. The telescope takes its name after Edwin Hubble, an astronomer who has contributed immensely to our understanding of the workings of the universe.

The Hubble Telescope transmits over 140 GB of data every week

In 1990, after nearly twenty years of research and building, the Hubble Telescope was deployed to low Earth orbit by the space shuttle, *Discovery*.

The telescope is powered by two large solar panels. The telescope is designed in such a way that any repairs are carried out in space by astronauts. The telescope captures images and transmits them back to Earth.

The James Webb Space Telescope (JWST) that is jointly being designed by the ESA, NASA and the Canadian Space Agency is set to be launched into space in 2019 and will offer better resolution than even the Hubble Space Telescope.

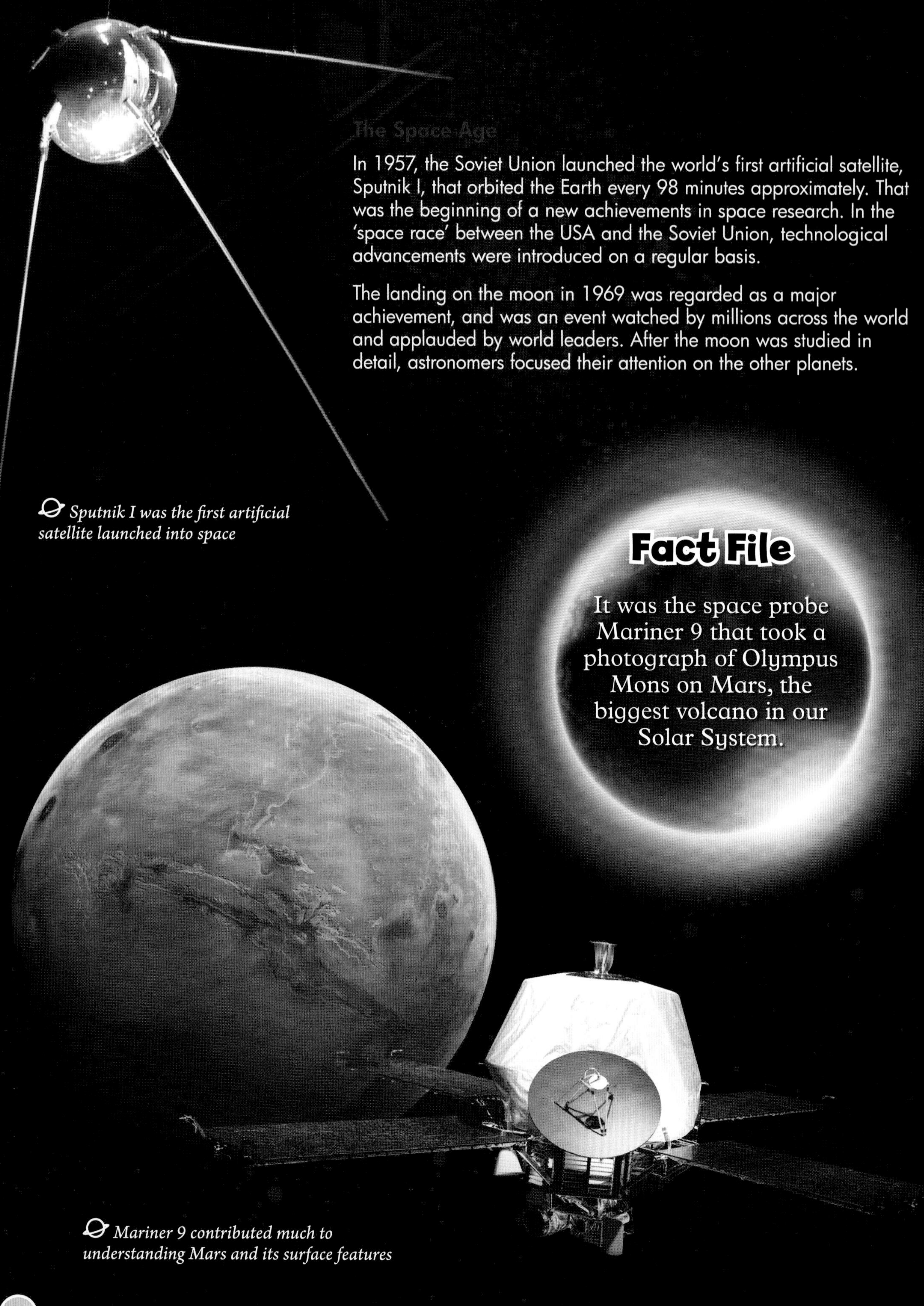

The Space Age

In 1957, the Soviet Union launched the world's first artificial satellite, Sputnik I, that orbited the Earth every 98 minutes approximately. That was the beginning of a new achievements in space research. In the 'space race' between the USA and the Soviet Union, technological advancements were introduced on a regular basis.

The landing on the moon in 1969 was regarded as a major achievement, and was an event watched by millions across the world and applauded by world leaders. After the moon was studied in detail, astronomers focused their attention on the other planets.

Sputnik I was the first artificial satellite launched into space

Fact File

It was the space probe Mariner 9 that took a photograph of Olympus Mons on Mars, the biggest volcano in our Solar System.

Mariner 9 contributed much to understanding Mars and its surface features

Space probes

A space probe is a specially designed device that can travel through space and collect and transmit information that can be useful for scientists and astronomers. After Sputnik I, the probe Explorer I was sent into space by the USA. The success of these early probes prompted scientists to then send them to the planets in our Solar System.

Mariner 2 became the first space probe to study another planet. In 1962 it flew past Venus and confirmed what astronomers had already assumed – Venus is a very hot planet.

Three years later in 1965, Mariner 4 flew past Mars and became the first space probe to take a picture of the planet.

In 1971, Mariner 9 was sent to Mars and became the first probe to orbit a planet.

NASA has succeeded in sending at least one probe to study all eight planets in our Solar System as well as the dwarf planet, Pluto.

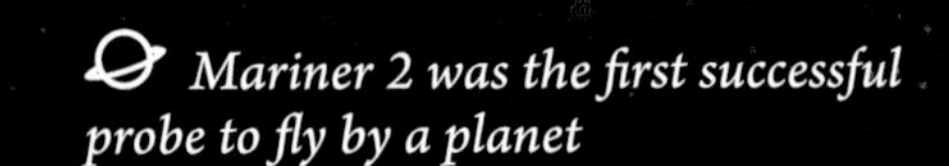

Mariner 2 was the first successful probe to fly by a planet

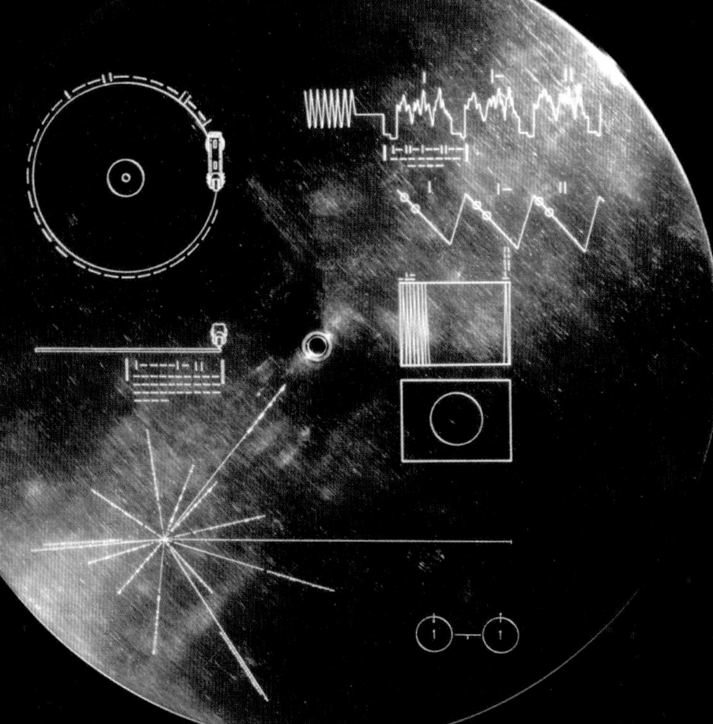

Beyond the Solar System

Among the most sophisticated probes ever designed are the twin spacecraft Voyager 1 and 2, tasked with exploring not just our immediate neighbourhood but far beyond. Launched in 1977, the spacecraft have been travelling for decades, visiting Jupiter, Saturn, Uranus and Neptune, and later exploring realms previously never imagined.

Voyager 1 has traveled the farthest distance of any object made by man, and has now gone beyond the edge of the Solar System. Both Voyager 1 and Voyager 2 carry a greeting message on a playable gold phonograph record if they were to encounter any form of intelligent life.

The Voyager Golden Record is 12 inches in diameter and has sounds and images of Earth

PLANETS OF OUR SOLAR SYSTEM

The four planets closest to the Sun, namely Mercury, Venus, Earth and Mars, are referred to as terrestrial planets or rocky planets. The planets beyond the asteroid belt, Jupiter and Saturn, are called gas giants, while Uranus and Neptune are known as ice giants.

MERCURY

VENUS

EARTH

MARS

Terrestrial Planets

Terrestrial planets have solid surfaces and a core made up of metal. These planets also have common features on the surface like craters, mountains, canyons and volcanoes. They are believed to have formed from accumulation of material from the gas and dust cloud, along with the Sun and other planets. The Sun collected nearly all of the dust and debris in the cloud while the rest of the material formed the planets. 'Planetesimals' refer to the rocky fragments in the early Solar System that were precursors of the formation of planets.

The lighter gases like hydrogen and helium were pushed farther from the Sun to form the giant planets. Heavier elements like iron and nickel accumulated as the cores of the four terrestrial planets. After the cores were formed, other material accumulated around them. Those materials that did not form planets remained in the Solar System as debris. The asteroid belt is a notable region of icy and rocky bodies considered to be the remnants of planet formation.

Earth is Unique

Among the terrestrial planets, Mercury is the smallest and Earth the largest. Despite not being the closest to the Sun, Venus is the hottest planet because its atmosphere traps heat and radiation. Among the planets in the Solar System, Earth is the only one to have accumulated enough liquid water and to possess conditions which support complex life forms. Life here developed through the process of evolution over millions of years.

Earth is the largest of the terrestrial planets and supports complex life

Gas and Ice Giants

The four outer planets; Jupiter, Saturn, Uranus and Neptune, are classified as 'giants' and vary greatly in size and composition from the terrestrial planets. All four planets have rings around them.

Initially all four planets beyond the asteroid belt were classified as gas giants, because the term originally referred to their gigantic size. However, only Jupiter and Saturn are made up almost entirely of hydrogen and helium, the two lightest elements. Heavier elements make up from 3 to 13 percent of their mass and are mostly concentrated in the centre to form a small core. The two planets are also referred to as 'failed stars' because they contain the basic elements that make up a star.

Scientists have estimated that Jupiter and Saturn initially formed like terrestrial planets. Over time, they grew in size by accumulating more of the hydrogen and helium from the gas cloud during the formation of the Solar System. Studies have revealed that the gas giants formed relatively quickly, possibly quite soon after the Sun was formed.

Uranus and Neptune are classified as ice giants because they are made up of heavier elements than hydrogen and helium, such as carbon, nitrogen, oxygen and sulphur. Similar to how gas giants formed, Uranus and Neptune initially had large rocky cores that gathered more material over millions of years. The outer layer of these planets is similar to that of the gas giants.

The gas giants are large and massive compared to the terrestrial planets

Fact File

The term 'gas giant' was coined in 1952 by science fiction writer James Blish to refer to all four giant planets in the Solar System.

MERCURY

Mercury is the smallest planet in our Solar System and the closest to the Sun. Named after the swift Roman deity who was the messenger of the Gods, Mercury is the fastest among all planets. It completes an orbit of the Sun in just 88 days. Mercury is smaller even than two moons in our Solar System.

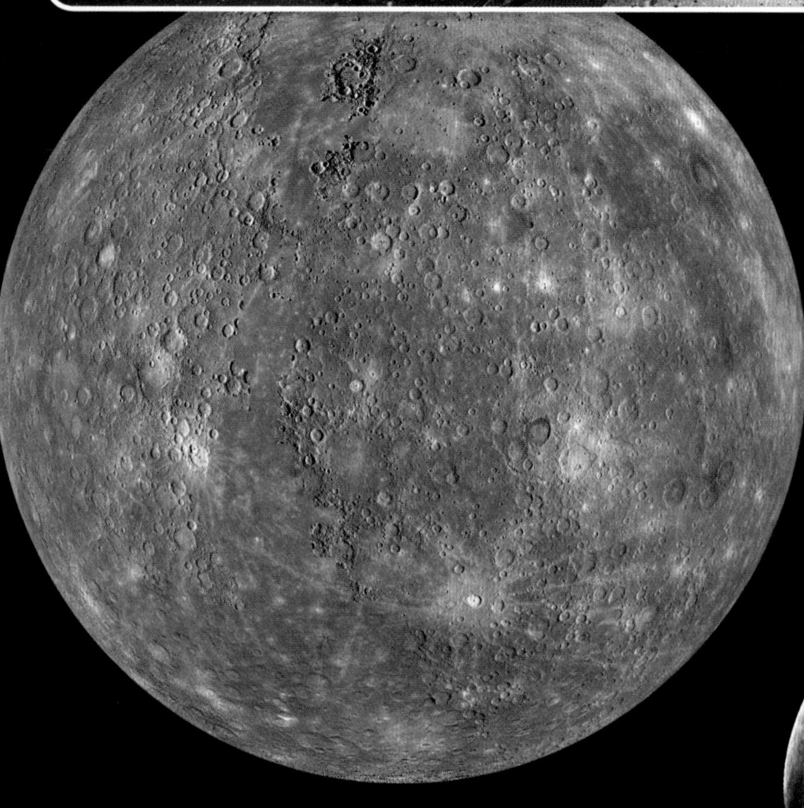

Since Mercury is very close to the Sun, it is only possible to observe the planet at dawn or in the evening when the Sun is not as bright. For around 13 times every century it is possible to see Mercury cross the Sun's face. This event is called a 'transit'. Mercury has been known since early times. Both Galileo Galilee and Thomas Harriott viewed the planet through a telescope.

After Earth, Mercury is the densest planet in our Solar System. Mercury has a metallic core that makes up nearly 80 percent of the planet's radius. The outer crust has smooth plains with cliffs strewn around.

Mercury has a core that makes up 80 percent of the planet

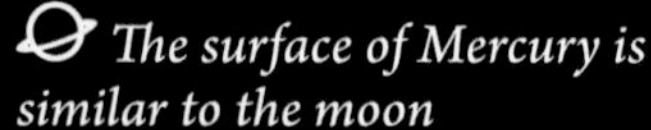

The surface of Mercury is similar to the moon

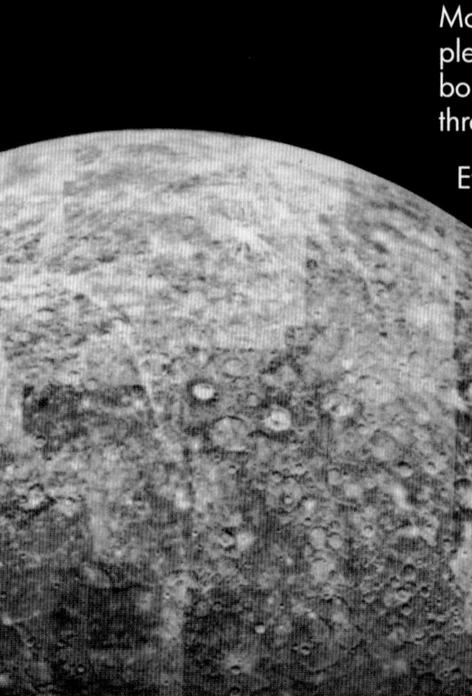

Extremes on the Planet

The surface of Mercury is similar to that of the Moon, with a barren landscape covered with plenty of craters. The planet was constantly bombarded by meteorites and comets throughout its early formation period.

Even though Mercury is very close to the Sun, the temperature here can fluctuate between 800 degrees Fahrenheit (425°C) and -290 degrees Fahrenheit (-180°C). The reasons for the wide range in temperature are that Mercury has an eccentric orbit – it can orbit as close as 47 million kilometres from the sun to as far as 70 million kilometres from it. Mercury also has no atmosphere to regulate the temperature on the surface.

Viewing Mercury

The Hubble Telescope can't be used for observing Mercury as it is too close to the Sun for its delicate components. Pointing the telescope at Mercury would heat up and destroy its sensitive instruments. Only two spacecraft have visited the planet because of the technical difficulties involved. As a result, Mercury has been studied less thoroughly than the other planets.

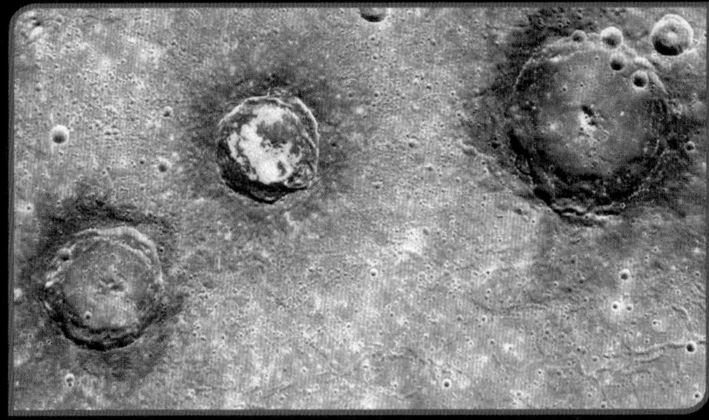

Close-up of craters on Mercury

Fact File

For a spacecraft to travel to Mercury requires more rocket fuel than what would be needed for it to escape the Solar System completely.

Mercury Missions

Mariner 10: This was the first spacecraft to visit Mercury and in 1974 flew past the planet three times, revealing details about the planet's surface features such as craters and cliffs. Mariner 10 ran out of fuel soon after its close approach and its operation had to be shut down.

MESSENGER: This was the second mission to study Mercury, launched by NASA in 2004. MESSENGER stands for MErcury Surface, Space ENvironment, GEochemistry and Ranging. It first flew past the planet in 2008 and then entered into an orbit around Mercury studying its different features and providing valuable information and extensive images until its mission ended in 2015.

MESSENGER orbited Mercury from 2009 to 2015, providing images and data

VENUS

Even though Venus is the second-closest planet to the Sun, it is actually the hottest planet in our Solar System. Venus is named after the Roman Goddess of Love and Beauty. Venus is Earth's closest neighbour and is approximately the same size as the Earth.

Discovery and Understanding of Venus

In earlier times Venus was known as both the 'morning star' and the 'evening star' because people assumed Venus to be two different bodies. Galileo Galilee, who extensively studied all the different planets, observed that Venus exhibits phases just like the Moon. This was clear evidence that Venus orbited around the Sun and not the Earth as had been assumed until then. Like Mercury, Venus also transits in front of the Sun, enabling astronomers to better understand the planet.

The telescope helped reveal that Venus was not a star but a planet similar in size to Earth and with a thick atmosphere. People believed that Venus would be warmer than Earth but still habitable. When space probes visited the planet and provided details about the surface temperature of Venus, this theory was dismissed. Venus was not only too hot for living things to thrive, it was much hotter even, than Mercury, located closer to the Sun.

The temperature on Venus reaches up to 880 degrees Fahrenheit (470°C) - hot enough to melt lead! The reason for Venus's high temperature is its thick atmosphere consisting mainly of carbon dioxide and clouds full of sulphuric acid droplets. This atmosphere traps heat from the Sun and prevents it from escaping. However, on the top layers of Venus's atmosphere the temperature is similar to that on Earth's surface.

The surface of Venus is too hot to support life

Venus and Earth are neighbours and similar in size

Venus Rotation

Venus has an unusual rotation, very different to that of the other planets. It rotates in an anticlockwise direction – the only other planet in our Solar System that does it is Uranus. Venus rotates very slowly around its axis. To give a comparison, Earth rotates around its axis in 1 day, while Venus takes 225 Earth days to complete a rotation.

Venus is seen as a dot on the Sun during its transit

Venus Missions

Several space missions have been sent to Venus to study and better understand the planet.

Mariner 2: This space probe launched by NASA was the first to successfully fly by Venus in 1962, and gathered early data about the conditions on Venus.

Venera: Several space probes in the Venera series were launched to Venus by the Soviet Union from 1961 onwards. In 1967, Venera 4 managed to assess the atmospheric conditions before it was destroyed.

Other space probes in the Venera and Mariner series have managed to successfully fly by Venus. Galileo, Magellan, Venus Express, Pioneer 1 and 2, Vega 1 and 2, and MESSENGER are spacecraft that have studied Venus and provided important data and photographs of the planet.

Fact File

Scientists have estimated that billions of years ago, Venus's atmosphere was similar to Earth's as it is today.

Venera I is the first of many in the series of Venera probes to study Venus

EARTH

Largest among the terrestrial planets, Earth is the third planet from the Sun and the only one known to support complex life. The name 'Earth' came about nearly 1000 years ago. Unlike the other planets that are named after Greek or Roman gods, the word is of English/Germanic origin and means 'ground.'

Earth's Atmosphere

The atmosphere is a layer of gases surrounding the planet and held in place by Earth's gravitational pull. It is this layer of gases and its composition that enables the formation and continuation of life. It is also responsible for shielding the surface from harmful ultraviolet radiation, cosmic rays and solar winds. Most meteoroids get burned up in the atmosphere before striking the surface, thus rendering them harmless. Planets without an atmosphere are often cratered by striking meteorites. The atmosphere is made up of nitrogen, oxygen, argon, carbon dioxide, water vapour and traces of a few other gases.

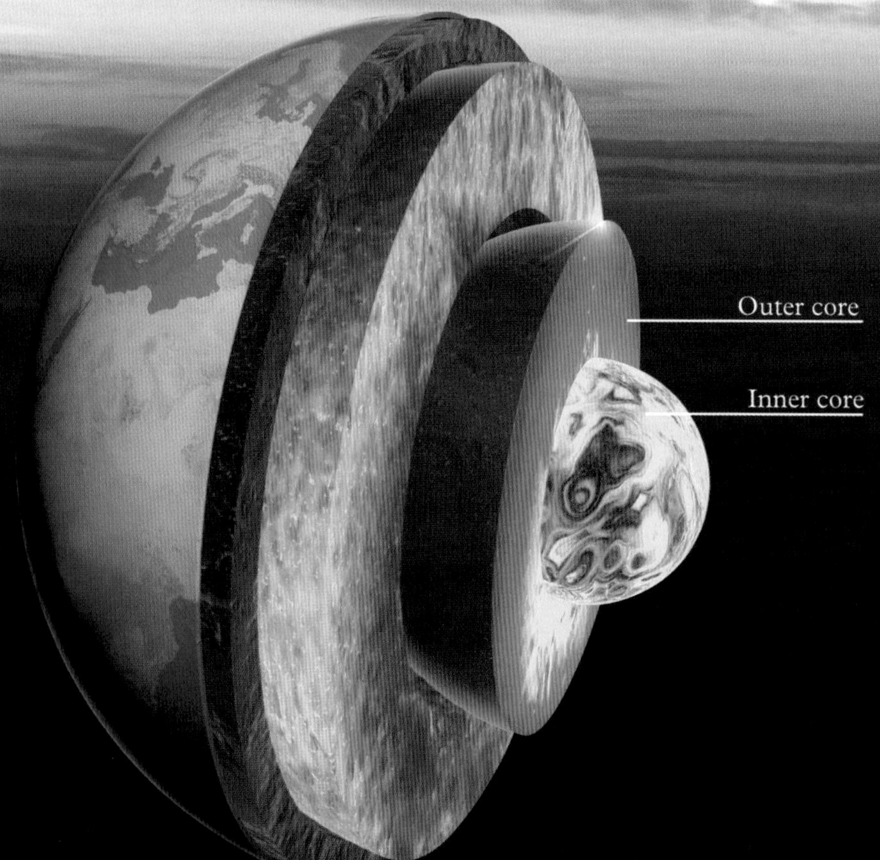

Earth's Composition

Earth has a hot core, a rocky mantle region and a thin crust upon which the oceans and continents are located. While the crust is the thinnest layer, immediately underneath it, the mantle, is the thickest, extending to a depth of 2890 kilometres. The core is filled with dense materials - mostly iron, with a small percentage of nickel.

The molten iron and nickel present in the Earth's outer core along with its rotation, gives rise to a magnetic field. It is this magnetic field that is responsible for making the needles in magnetic compasses point north. Interestingly, the Earth's magnetic field flips or reverses every 400,000 years. When this happens, the compass needles that currently point north, will instead point towards the south.

Life on Earth

Earth has favourable temperatures and pressure conditions, as well as a medley of chemical components, and an atmosphere, that collectively have made life possible and have enabled life to evolve here over millions of years. The famous Urey and Miller chemical experiment simulated conditions similar to early Earth and showed how amino acids (that form proteins) were produced when water, methane, ammonia and hydrogen were subjected to electric sparks. The formation of these amino acids and DNA would have been the precursors for the generation of life forms. A billion years after Earth formed, primitive organisms like bacteria developed. More complex life forms began to develop about 1.8 billion years ago. Humans only evolved about 5 to 7 million years ago.

Life evolved on Earth a billion years after it was formed

Moon

Earth has a single satellite, the Moon, that is located at a distance of around 239,000 miles. The Moon has a significant role in enabling Earth to support life. It moderates the wobble as the Earth spins on its axis and enables stable and predictable climate patterns. The Moon's gravitational pull is responsible for ocean tides that help cycle nutrients, necessary for life to flourish.

The Moon is the only celestial object in our Solar System that is prominently visible in clear detail and also where we have landed. The Moon is believed to have been formed from the Earth after the collision of a 'Mars-sized' object with the Earth.

Fact File

Did you know that the Moon is slowly moving away from the Earth at the rate of about an inch every year?

Have you wondered why we see the same side of the Moon all the time? The Moon orbits around the Earth at the same rate it rotates around its axis. The Moon's orbit around the Earth is also the reason why we see it go through phases. During the 'full moon' phase we see the hemisphere of the Moon facing us fully illuminated by the Sun. The 'new moon' phase is when the other side is in sunlight and it is night time on the hemisphere facing us.

The Moon had many active volcanoes, but they are all dormant now and have not erupted in a very long time.

Humans landed on the moon in 1969

MARS

Referred to as the 'Red Planet', Mars is a small planet bearing features like polar ice caps, vast stretches of deserts, canyons and massive craters similar to those found on the Earth and the Moon. It is among the many objects visible to the naked eye in the night sky.

Mars – Composition and Features

The reddish appearance of the planet is due to the presence of iron oxide on its surface. Mars is roughly half the size of the Earth and also has a tilt in its rotational axis, resulting in seasons. Looking through a telescope, it is possible to identify the polar ice caps as well as the changing features on the surface corresponding to seasonal variations. The thin atmosphere on Mars is made up almost entirely of carbon dioxide, with a small percentage of argon and nitrogen, as well as trace amounts of oxygen, water vapour and methane.

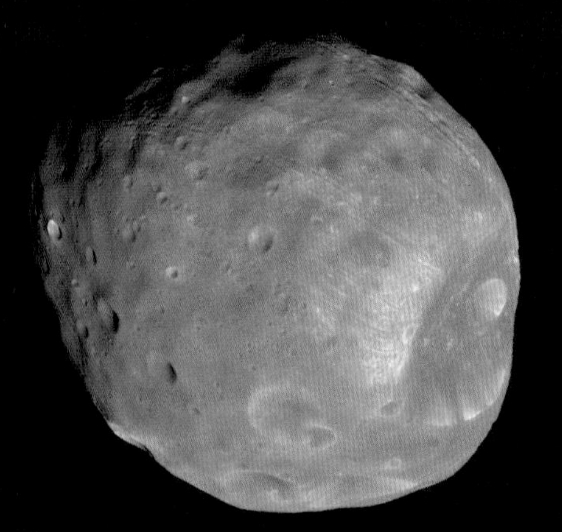

PHOBOS

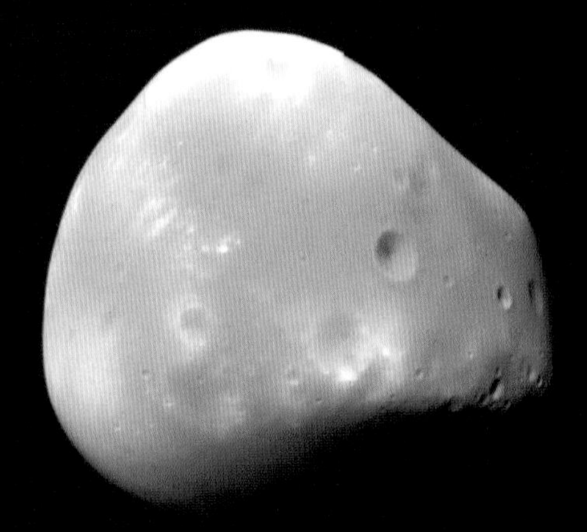

DEIMOS

Moons

Mars has two irregularly-shaped moons, Phobos and Deimos, both of which were discovered in 1877 by the American astronomer, Asaph Hall. The two moons were named after the sons of the God of War, known as Ares by the Greeks and Mars by the Romans. They are rich in rocks and ice, are heavily cratered, and are even believed by some to be asteroids captured into Mars's orbit.

The two moons of Mars are the smallest and hence least well illuminated in the Solar System. This might explain why they weren't discovered until the nineteenth century.

Phobos orbits Mars at a distance of 6,000 kilometres. No other moon in the Solar System orbits so close to a planet. One of the most prominent features of Phobos is a crater extending for 10 kilometres, about half the moon's width.

Fact File

Mars is the home of the tallest mountain in the Solar System, Olympus Mons, a volcano more than two times the height of Mount Everest.

Viking I was the first of the two Mars orbiters and landers launched in 1975

Mars Missions

Several types of spacecraft have been sent to Mars including orbiters, landers and rovers. They have been launched by different countries all to study the planet in more detail. The earliest and most significant among them was Mariner 4 that captured 22 photos of the red planet in 1965. The photos revealed a bleak, rocky and cratered surface that showed the reality of the planet's surface that was long believed to host living organisms like Earth. Many other missions followed, such as Viking 1 and 2, Mars Pathfinder, Mars Odyssey, Spirit, Opportunity, Mars Reconnaissance Orbiter, Phoenix and Curiosity. Findings reveal that the planet is more complex than previously thought and detailed research will eventually uncover clues about its past and also whether it would one day be possible for humans to inhabit the planet.

The Martian landscape is dry and barren like a desert

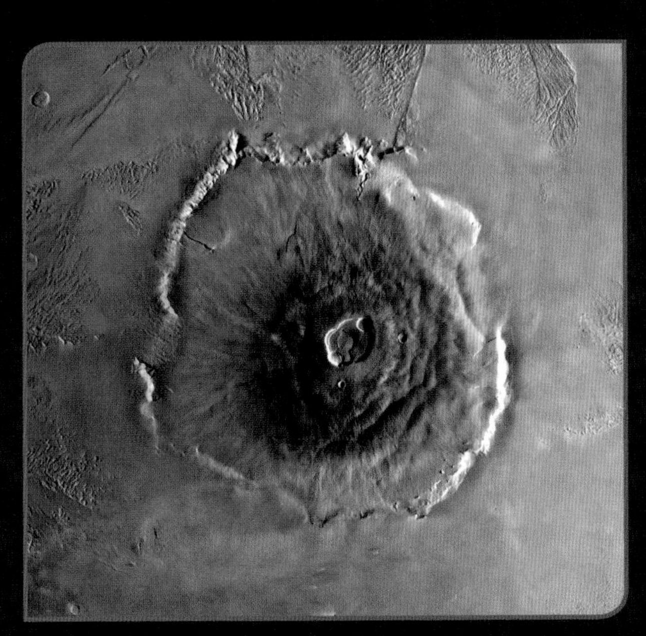

Olympus Mons on Mars is the tallest volcano in the solar System

Mars Settlement

For decades people have been debating the idea of human colonies settling on Mars in the near future. NASA has already begun preparations for sending people to Mars in the 2030s. Mars One and Space X are private organizations that, after years of preparations, are planning to send humans for permanent settlement on Mars and establishing colonies there.

JUPITER

The fifth planet from the sun, Jupiter is the largest planet in our Solar System and is the second brightest object in the night sky, and hence has been known to people since early times. It was the Romans who gave the planet its name, and it was named after their God of Sky and Thunder. Since Jupiter is made up mostly of the gases hydrogen and helium, it does not have a defined solid surface.

Jupiter is the largest planet in the Solar System

The Solar System's Giant

After the Sun, Jupiter is the largest heavenly body in our Solar System and is classified as a 'gas giant'. It is so big that it could accommodate all the other planets within it. Jupiter's characteristic appearance of white and red stripes is due to the brown, yellow, and white clouds found in its atmosphere. Jupiter has three faint rings that were only discovered in 1979 by the Voyager I spacecraft.

Moons of Jupiter

Jupiter has been observed with the naked eye since very early times. However, not much was known about its moons until Galileo Galilee and Simon Marius independently discovered the four largest moons of Jupiter. They are also know as the Galilean satellites, in honour of Galileo Galilee. They were named Io, Europa, Ganymede and Callisto, based on Simon Marius's suggestion. Ganymede is the largest moon in our Solar System, much bigger than Mercury and nearly three-quarters the size of Mars. Jupiter has 69 known moons, of which 53 have been officially named. Most of the moons were discovered in the 21st century.

NOTABLE MOONS

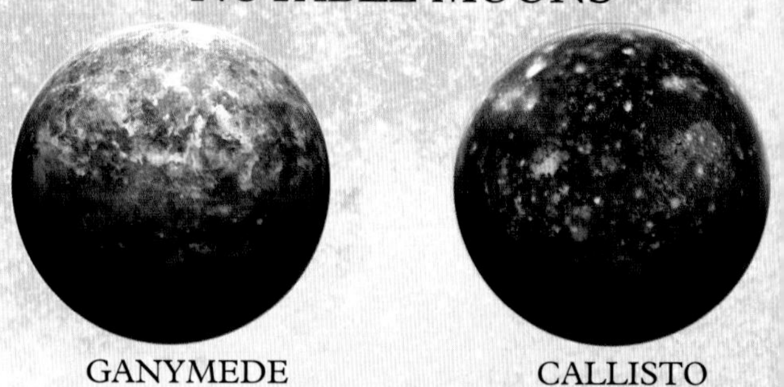

GANYMEDE CALLISTO

IO EUROPA

Fact File

More than 1300 Earths could fit inside Jupiter. In fact, Jupiter is more like a star based on its composition of hydrogen and helium.

The Great Red Spot

One of the most prominent features of Jupiter is the Great Red Spot, a rapidly spinning storm that has been raging for a long time. It is estimated to be about the size of Earth.

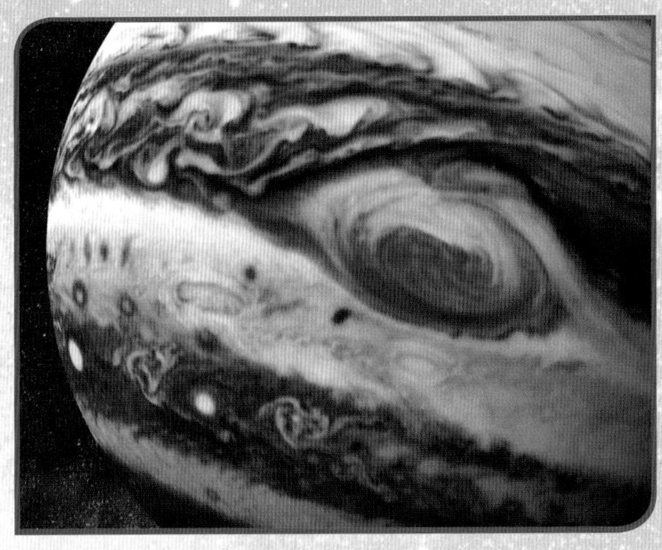

The Great Red Spot on Jupiter is a storm that has been raging for hundreds of years

Space Missions to Jupiter

Pioneer 10: The first spacecraft to fly past Jupiter and take close-up shots of the planet and its moons in 1973.

Pioneer 11: This spacecraft arrived in 1974 and took photographs of the Great Red Spot and the polar regions of the planet.

Voyager 1 and 2: Both Voyager 1 and 2 approached Jupiter in 1979 and together they revealed details about the planet's rings, its minor moons, the storm in the Great Red Spot and the four major moons.

Ulysses: This spacecraft flew near Jupiter's North Pole to measure its magnetic activity. However, it had no cameras, so no photographs were taken on this mission.

Cassini: On its way to Saturn, Cassini flew by Jupiter and provided the best resolution photographs, so far, of the planet.

New Horizons: On its way to Pluto, this spacecraft went past Jupiter and studied many features, including the Great Red Spot and Jupiter's inner moons.

Galileo: The first spacecraft to orbit around Jupiter after arriving in 1995, and remained in orbit for 7 years, making many important discoveries about Jupiter and its moons.

Juno: Launched in 2011, Juno entered into Jupiter's orbit in 2016 and has been helpful in better understanding about the gravity, atmosphere and winds on the surface of the planet.

Jupiter Icy Moon Explorer: The European Space Agency will launch this explorer in 2022 to study Jupiter's moons and it is expected to arrive near Jupiter in 2030.

The Juno spacecraft arrived at Jupiter in 2016 to study the planet's surface

SATURN

Adorned with thousands of rings around it, Saturn is unique among the planets in the Solar System. It is also the farthest planet that is visible to the naked eye in the night sky. Named after the Roman God of Agriculture, Saturn is the sixth planet from the Sun.

Discovery of Saturn

It was Galileo Galilee, the Italian astronomer, who first viewed the planet through a telescope way back in 1610. He was greatly surprised and confused by its odd appearance, which changed with both the Earth's revolution and Saturn's tilt and orbit. It was in the year 1659 that another astronomer, Christian Huygens, correctly deduced that Saturn had rings.

Galileo Galilee observed Saturn more than 400 years ago, but his telescope did not clearly reveal the rings.

Saturn's Spectacular Rings

Saturn is not the only planet with rings – Jupiter, Neptune and Uranus have them too – but none are as prominent or remarkable as the rings around Saturn. Even though seven distinct rings have been recognised around Saturn, each ring consists of thousands of thinner ringlets made of fragments of comets and asteroids that broke apart before reaching the planet's surface. The rings extend to 175,000 miles from the planet, but interestingly, the thickness of the rings is only about one kilometre.

Fact File

All of Saturn's moons are named after Titans in Greek mythology as well as giants in Nordic, Gallic and Inuit mythology.

Space Missions to Saturn

Pioneer 11: The first space probe to study Saturn, launched in 1973 and passing close to the planet in 1979. It took a close-up picture of Saturn and revealed a ring that was previously not discovered.

Voyager 1: In 1980, Voyager 1 flew close to Saturn and took a series of pictures of the planet, its stunning rings, and one of its moons, Titan.

Voyager 2: In 1981, a year after Voyager 1's visit, Voyager 2 approached the planet and flew close to several of Saturn's moons.

Cassini/Huygens: Cassini/Huygens spacecraft was the first to be designed for studying Saturn in detail and not just as a flyby mission like the others. It arrived in 2004 and the Huygens probe was dropped on Titan while Cassini provided details about Saturn, its rings and moons.

Cassini is one of the largest interplanetary spacecraft built so far, weighing around 6 tons.

Saturn is made up of hydrogen and helium and is the lightest planet in our Solar System.

NOTABLE MOONS

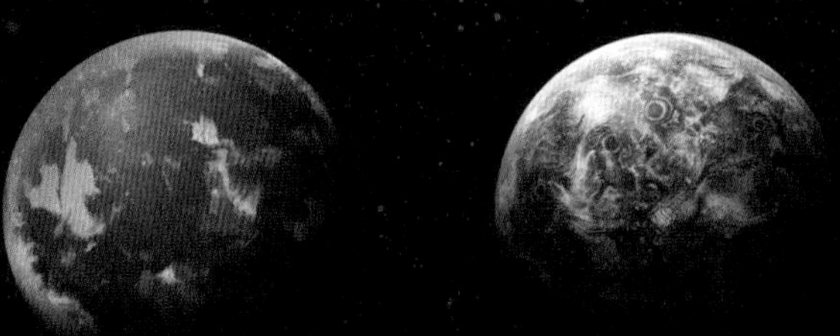

TITAN · RHEA · IAPETUS

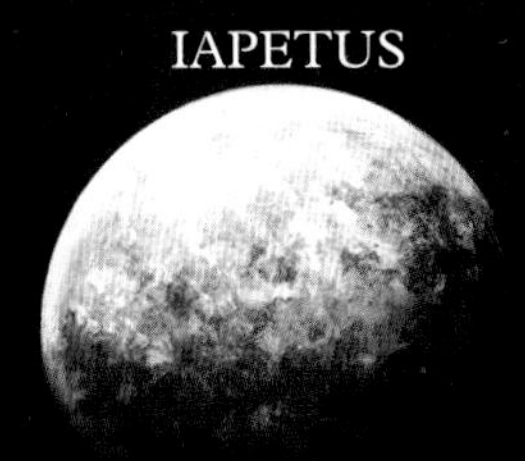

DIONE · TETHYS · ENCELADUS

Moons of Saturn

There are 53 named moons of Saturn and others that are yet to be confirmed. Saturn's largest moon, Titan, is bigger than the planet Mercury. Titan alone makes up 94 percent of the weight of all the moons of Saturn. Scientists are studying Titan for the possibility of supporting life, as it has a dense atmosphere with nitrogen, water (as ice) rocky material, and hydrocarbon lakes, similar to early Earth. Other studied moons of Saturn include Enceladus, Mimas, Hyperion, Tethys, Rhea, Dione, and Iapetus.

URANUS

Uranus is the seventh planet from the Sun and third largest in our Solar System. It is also the first planet that was found using a telescope in 1781, and although previously observed, it was mistaken for a star and not recorded as a planet by any astronomer. Uranus is said to have some of the brightest clouds in the Solar System.

Discovery of Uranus

William Herschel discovered Uranus through a telescope in 1781, but it was 2 years later that Uranus was finally conferred the title of a planet. Herschel initially thought it was a comet, but observations by other astronomers revealed its orbiting pattern beyond that of Saturn. The planet is named after the Greek god of the sky, a name that was agreed upon nearly 70 years after it was discovered.

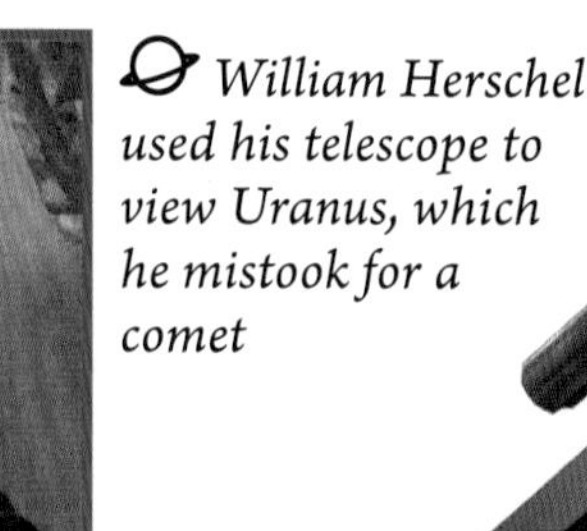

William Herschel used his telescope to view Uranus, which he mistook for a comet

The Retrograde Planet

Although Uranus has not been studied as extensively as Saturn or Jupiter, certain features have been discovered that are unique to it. Uranus has a unique rotational axis that is nearly parallel to that of the plane of the Solar System. It is believed that this might be the result of a collision with a large object about the size of Earth. Uranus also rotates in a direction opposite to that of the other planets, and is hence referred to as a 'retrograde' planet. Uranus is surrounded by 13 faint rings, not as clearly visible as those of Saturn.

Uranus is known as an 'ice giant' owing to its composition – methane, water, and ammonia present in the form of a thick fluid. The blue-green appearance of the planet is mainly due to the presence of methane in the atmosphere. No spacecraft would be able to pass through Uranus's atmosphere without getting destroyed by the extreme pressure and temperature conditions. The planet is also the coldest, even though Neptune is farther from the sun than Uranus. Icy winds at very high speed are common on the planet's surface.

Moons of Uranus

Uranus has 27 known moons. The five best-known moons are Titania, Miranda, Ariel, Umbriel and Oberon. Titania is the largest moon, yet its size is less than that of our planet's moon. Almost all the moons are made up of roughly equal percentages of ice and rock.

NOTABLE MOONS

TITANIA

OBERON

UMBRIEL

ARIEL

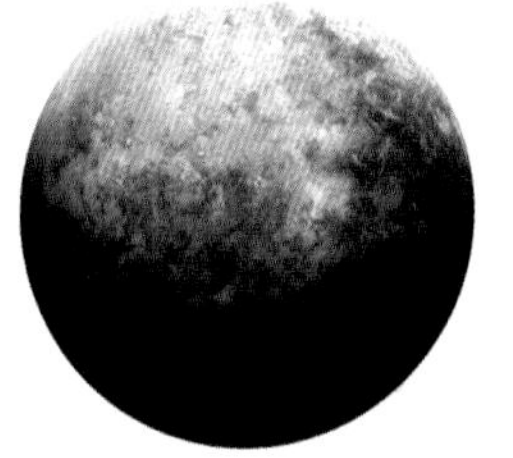

MIRANDA

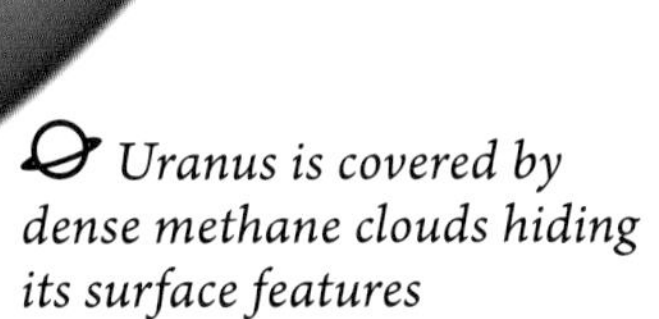

Uranus is covered by dense methane clouds hiding its surface features

Space Missions to Uranus

Voyager 2: It remains the only spacecraft to have flown past Uranus in 1986, on its way to Neptune and beyond. It investigated the structure, chemical nature and weather patterns of the planet. The photographs taken by Voyager 2 show a plain planet with no remarkable features. Apart from investigating Neptune's largest moons, the spacecraft also identified 10 previously unknown ones.

A space mission to Uranus is planned sometime between 2020 and 2023. The spacecraft would take around 13 years to reach the planet.

Fact File

While other satellites are named after Greek and Roman gods, Uranus's moons are named after characters from the works of Shakespeare and Alexander Pope.

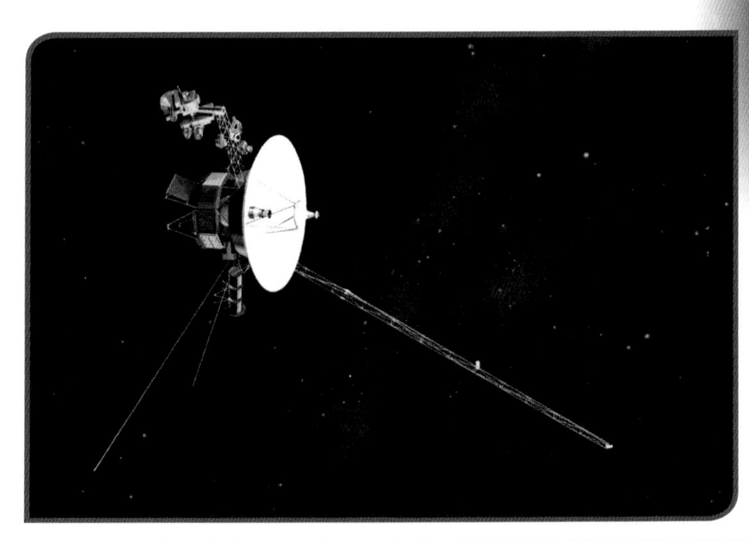

Voyager 2 flew past Uranus in 1986, the only craft to visit the planet

NEPTUNE

Neptune is the eighth planet in our Solar System and the farthest from the Sun. Among the planets identified, Neptune is the only one that was predicted by mathematical calculations rather than by observation through telescopes. The blue appearance of the planet helped earn its name 'Neptune,' the Roman God of the Sea.

Discovery of Neptune

Due to its extreme distance from Earth, Neptune is not visible to the naked eye. Galileo Galilee observed Neptune with his telescope but he mistook it for a star. It was Joseph le Verrier, a French mathematician, who proposed not only the position but also the approximate mass of another planet that seemed to be causing disturbances to Uranus's orbit. It was after his predictions that Neptune was identified for the first time in 1846 in the Berlin Observatory.

Neptune, along with Uranus, is classified as an ice giant as the planet is mostly made up of ice and rock. The ice present in the planet is mostly made up of ammonia, methane and water. Hydrogen and helium make up the atmosphere of Neptune. Even though Neptune is farther from the Sun than Uranus, the surface temperatures of both planets are roughly equal. This is believed to be because due to internal heating.

Joseph Le Verrier predicted the eight planet Neptune through calculations

Neptune is an ice giant and viewed as a vivid blue coloured planet

Neptune's Physical Features

The blue colour of the planet is due to the presence of methane in its atmosphere. Similar to Jupiter's Great Red Spot, Neptune has a 'Great Dark Spot'. This Earth-sized oval storm was identified by Voyager 2 during its visit to the planet. The storm spins in a direction opposite to the rotation of the planet is so intense that the winds are estimated at a speed of 1200 kilometres per hour. This is much stronger than the winds on Jupiter. However, unlike the Great Red Spot on Jupiter that has been continuing for centuries, Neptune's storm lasts for a much shorter time.

Like Jupiter, Saturn and Uranus, Neptune also has a ring system, although it is much fainter. The rings are thought to be made of coated ice particles that give out a reddish hue. Scientists have discovered that the rings around Neptune are unstable.

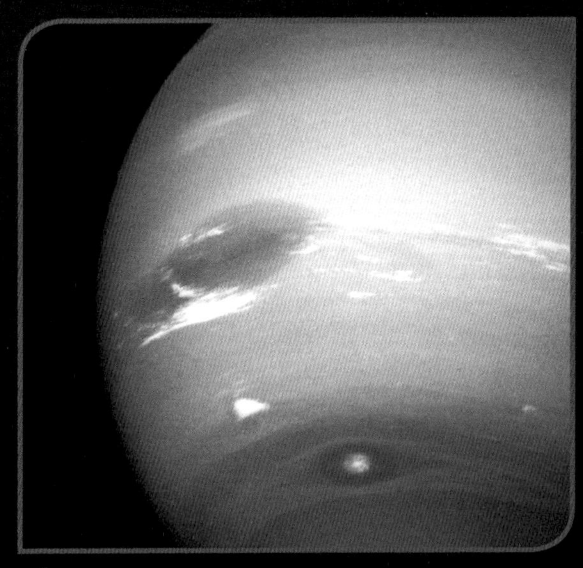

The Great Dark Spot is a raging storm on the windy planet

Neptune's Moons

There are 14 known moons of Neptune, of which Triton, the largest of its moons, was the one to be discovered first. Scientists believe that Triton was originally a dwarf planet that was captured into orbit around Neptune.

Triton is the largest among Neptune's 14 moons

Fact File

Among Neptune's moons, Triton rotates in a direction opposite to all the other moons.

Neptune Missions

Voyager 2: This is the only spacecraft to visit Neptune. The spacecraft flew about 4800 kilometres above the North Pole of the planet in 1989. It was previously assumed that Neptune did not have any disturbances in its atmosphere because it was too cold but the findings revealed by Voyager 2 showed that Neptune had large longterm storms as well as the fastest winds in the Solar System. It also captured photos of Neptune's moon, Triton. Voyager 2 also found a faint ring system around Neptune and new moons that were previously undiscovered.

DWARF PLANETS

The term 'dwarf planet' is relatively new and is used for classifying objects in our Solar System that are not asteroids but also do not qualify as planets. Under the new system of classification, Pluto has been redesignated as a dwarf planet.

PLUTO

ERIS

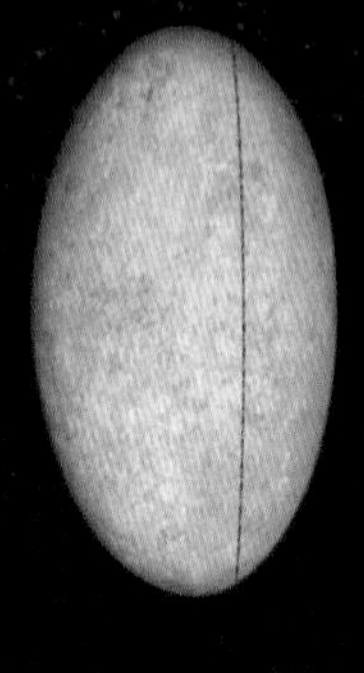

HAUMEA

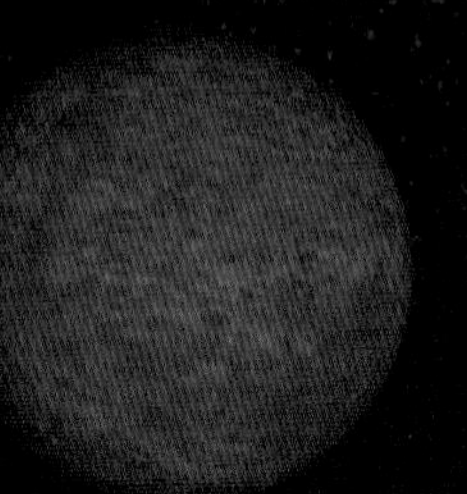

MAKEMAKE

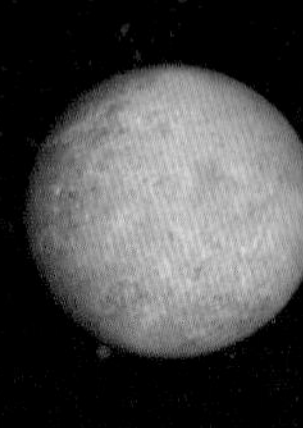

CERES

Location of Dwarf Planets

Beyond the orbit of Neptune is a disc-shaped region (Kuiper Belt) of icy objects and comets that form the outer realm of the Solar System. This region is believed to contain thousands of bodies which are larger than 100 kilometres in size and they are thought to be the remnants of the Solar System after the planets formed. It is here that Pluto and the other dwarf planets (except Ceres) are found. They are collectively referred to as 'trans-Neptunian objects'.

There are billions of objects in the Kuiper Belt of varied sizes

Fact File

Pluto's eccentric orbit brings it closer to the Sun than Neptune every few years. The last time this happened was between 1979 and 1999.

Missions to Kuiper Belt

Given the limitations of viewing Kuiper Belt objects clearly from Earth, scientists depend on close-up observations from spacecraft. New Horizons, a spacecraft that visited Pluto, will also pass through the Kuiper Belt. It will observe objects in the Kuiper Belt and provide a better understanding of how dwarf planets form there, and possibly spot new dwarf planet candidates in the region.

Classifying Dwarf Planets

In order to be classified as a dwarf planet, a celestial object has to have enough mass as well as gravity to assume a round or nearly round shape like a planet. It must also travel around the Sun in a specific orbit. The path of a dwarf planet's orbit is usually strewn with comets and asteroids. However, a planet has a clear path and orbit around the Sun. While scientists estimate that there could be several dwarf planets in the outer Solar System, so far only five have been identified and officially named. They are: Pluto, Ceres, Eris, Haumea, Makemake.

CHARON

Pluto

Until recently Pluto had been the ninth planet in our Solar System. Following the discovery of other bodies similar to Pluto, in 2006 Pluto was officially redesignated as a dwarf planet. It was named after the Greek god of the underworld.

Pluto's Moons

Pluto has 5 moons in total – Charon, Nix, Hydra, Kerberos and Styx. The moons of Pluto are thought to have formed after a planet-sized body crashed into it. Charon is the biggest of Pluto's moons and nearly half its size. Charon was discovered in 1978 by the American astronomer, James Christy. Recent high resolution photographs of Charon show that the surface has craters, mountains, landslides and canyons.

Clyde Tombaugh discovered Pluto in 1930

Pluto Missions

New Horizons: NASA's New Horizons, a spacecraft no bigger than a piano, was launched in 2006. It reached Pluto in 2015 and has been taking photographs and making measurements to better understand the dwarf planet and its moons. The mission was designed not only to study Pluto and its satellites but also other Kuiper belt objects.

New Horizons spacecraft was launched to study Pluto, its moons and Kuiper Belt objects

Discovery of Pluto

Pluto was discovered in 1930 by the American astronomer, Clyde Tombaugh. Pluto is smaller than our moon and located at a distance about 40 times that of Earth from the Sun. Owing to its distance, Pluto is extremely cold, with temperatures in the range of -375 to -470 degrees Fahrenheit (-225°C to -270°C). It has been estimated that Pluto might have ice volcanoes – the kind that spout out a cold slush of water, ice and gases. Pluto also exhibits retrograde rotation, that is, it spins in an anticlockwise direction like Uranus and Venus.

Eris

Eris is a dwarf planet close in size to Pluto and only slightly smaller. It is also the heaviest dwarf planet and farthest from the Sun. The dwarf planet has been named after the Greek goddess of disharmony. Eris is approximately three times farther from the Sun than Pluto and, not surprisingly, it is a frozen planet. It appears grey in colour and has a single moon called Dysnomia.

Fact File

Eris is located at a distance of approximately 10 billion kilometres from the Sun! Eris takes 557 Earth years to complete one orbit around the Sun.

Eris is slightly smaller than Pluto, though it was originally thought to be larger

HAUMEA

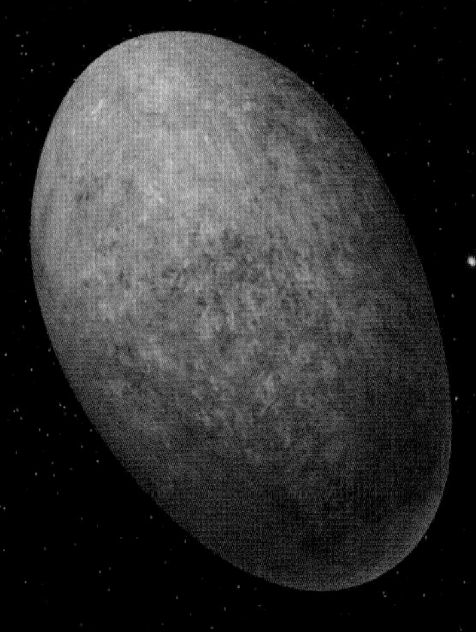

Haumea's odd shape is due to its very fast rotation

Haumea

Haumea is not only unique for its shape, but also for being the fastest rotating object in the Solar System known to us. Haumea spins so quickly that it completes one rotation in just 4 hours. It is this fast spinning motion that gives it its unique elongated shape. Scientists have estimated that Haumea is about the same size as Pluto.

Haumea has two small, irregularly-shaped moons. It is believed that a collision that occurred billions of years ago, is responsible for the rapid spinning of Haumea.

Haumea is named after the Hawaiian goddess of fertility and childbirth. The two moons of Haumea are appropriately named after the two daughters of Haumea, Hi'iaka and Namaka. Even though Haumea and its moons were discovered in 2003, the official announcement of the discovery was only made in 2005.

Makemake and Pluto are the brightest objects in the Kuiper Belt

Makemake

Like Pluto and Haumea, Makemake is a dwarf planet found in the Kuiper Belt region of the outer Solar System. It was discovered in 2005 by a team of scientists. Makemake is smaller than Pluto and named after the god of fertility in Rapa Nui mythology.

Makemake was quite difficult to discover against the background of stars in the Milky Way. However, next to Pluto, Makemake is the brightest object in the Kuiper Belt. The discovery of Makemake and Eris paved the way for scientists to reconsider the definition of planets and coin a new term 'dwarf planet.'

MAKEMAKE

Ceres

Ceres is the only dwarf planet located in the inner Solar System, in the asteroid belt region between Mars and Jupiter. Ceres is named after the Roman god of harvest. Ceres is referred to as an 'embryonic planet' – a planet that started to form but didn't quite finish.

Ceres was discovered for the first time by Giuseppe Piazzi in 1801. For many years, it was thought to be nothing more than a big asteroid. Detailed studies revealed that it was much bigger and different from other asteroids in the asteroid belt.

Ceres possesses a rocky core and a mantle that is thought to be made of water in the form of ice. Based on estimates, Ceres could comprise as much as 25 percent water. If this is true, Ceres will have more water than Earth. The dwarf planet completes one full rotation in merely 9 hours, one of the shortest in the Solar System.

Giuseppe Piazzi identified Ceres in 1801, mistaking it for an asteroid

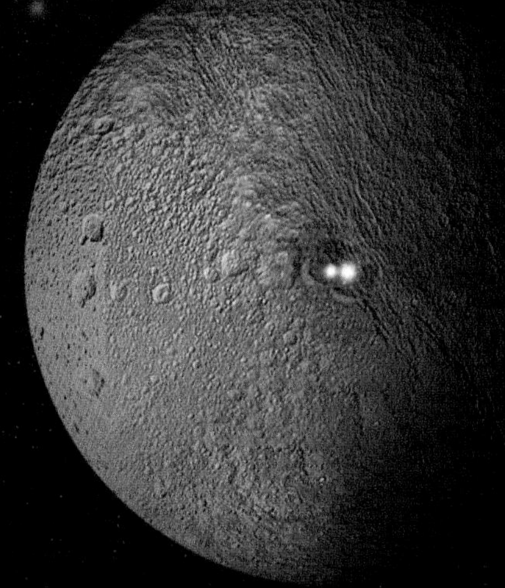

The Dawn Spacecraft was the first to land on a dwarf planet, Ceres

PLANETS OUTSIDE THE SOLAR SYSTEM

All planets outside our Solar System, orbiting stars other than our Sun, are referred to as 'exoplanets' or extra-solar planets. Even though astronomers have long predicted that the other stars in the universe would have planets orbiting them, it is only in the past few decades that they have been discovered.

51 Pegasi b is an exoplanet orbiting a star similar to the Sun

Fact File

Methuselah is the oldest exoplanet discovered so far. It is believed to have formed nearly 13 billion years ago. Earth is only 4.5 billion years old.

Discovery of Exoplanets

Humans have always been interested in knowing if life exists outside planet Earth. Scientists believed that finding stars similar to the Sun and planets located at an optimal distance from that star, could lead to the discovery of planets with the right conditions to host life on their surface.

It was in 1995 that the first exoplanet orbiting a star similar to the Sun was discovered. Given the name 51 Pegasi b, this planet was estimated to be about half the size of Jupiter and orbited quickly around the star. Ever since its exciting discovery, a race to find more exoplanets began. In a very short time, hundreds of other exoplanets were discovered, most of which were large gas giants like Jupiter.

The Kepler Space Telescope helps identify many exoplanets

The Kepler Space Telescope that was launched by NASA in 2009 started a new and improved phase of exoplanet hunting. Focusing on small patches of stars, the telescope identified thousands of planets. Along with the use of the Hubble Space Telescope and Spitzer Space Telescope, not only were more and more exoplanets identified, but so was their composition and type.

Types of Exoplanets

Scientists have identified many different types of exoplanets, varying in composition, size and uniqueness.

A pulsar planet orbits a pulsar - a rapidly rotating star that emits radiation continuously

Pulsar planet: This type of planet is found orbiting around a pulsar or rapidly-rotating neutron star. Before its discovery, scientists had never expected to find a planet near such a star, as they assumed it would have exploded or been destroyed.

Rogue planet: These are planets that are not bound to a star and were possibly ejected out of their system. Billions of rogue planets are thought to exist in the Milky Way.

A rogue planet either formed independently or was ejected from its system

Puffy planet: Gas giants that are large but not dense enough, are termed 'puffy planets'. Such a planet is found orbiting close to the star and thus has an inflated atmosphere. Six puffy planets have been identified so far.

Binary Star Orbiter: Planets that orbit one or both members of a binary (two) star system. Planets that orbit around triple and quadruple stars have also been discovered.

Techniques for Spotting Exoplanets

Scientists use 3 techniques to look for planets outside of our Solar System:

Direct Imaging: Very few planets are detected through this method because most planets that are too far from its star and do not reflect enough light to be visible. Planets directly viewed through powerful telescopes are usually bigger than Jupiter.

Transit: Just as it is possible for us to view Venus or Mercury when they 'transit' in front of the Sun, scientists can also identify a planet as it blocks light from a distant star. The Kepler Space Telescope and other sensitive instruments are used for observing planets in transit.

Wobble Method: The Solar System consists of a star (Sun) that is stationary and the planets orbiting around it. However, a large planet can exert gravitational pull on the star and cause it to 'wobble' slightly. Such small shifts in a star can be used to identify the presence and size of the planet. It is more useful for identifying larger planets than smaller ones. This method has helped identify hundreds of exoplanets.

Direct imaging is one of the techniques used for identifying exoplanets

THE FUTURE OF PLANET STUDY

The study of space, and in particular planets and their moons, has picked up tremendous pace in the twenty-first century. Developing advanced telescopes to study exoplanets is just one of the innovations made, as scientists prepare for the future of studying and better understanding the planets.

Telescopes of the Future

TESS: The Transiting Exoplanet Survey Satellite, called TESS, is a part of NASA's mission to find more exoplanets. When launched in 2018, this telescope will survey the brightest stars in the night sky for a period of two years. During this period, it is expected to scan at least 200,000 stars and identify any exoplanets orbiting them.

TESS will be employed in scanning the sky to identify exoplanets

Fact File

The James Webb Space Telescope is about the size of a tennis court and will be folded up to fit in the rocket for launch!

James Webb Space Telescope: This is a large space telescope that is expected be launched in 2019. With a better resolution capacity than the Hubble Telescope, it will help us study how solar systems like ours form, and identify planets capable of supporting life. The telescope will be able to study the atmospheres of exoplanets and also examine in greater detail the planets in our own Solar System. It will be useful for detecting previously unknown moons of the giant planets as well as for observing spectacular phenomena, like the giant storms, in better detail.

The James Webb Telescope, when launched, will provide a better picture of exoplanets

Giant Magellan Telescope: The Giant Magellan Telescope is currently under construction and expected to be completed by 2025. It will be a gigantic ground-based telescope that will be located in the Atacama Desert in Chile. The reason for this choice in location is that this area has the least amount of atmospheric and light pollution, and hence offers the best possible ground-based view of the night sky. The telescope will use seven of the largest mirrors ever made on Earth and will have a resolution power about ten times better than the Hubble Telescope. It will be used for studying exoplanets, like those orbiting the star Alpha Centauri, in better detail.

The Giant Magellan Telescope is being built in a location with the least atmospheric pollution for better resolution

Hunt for Earth-Like Exoplanets

The European Space Agency (ESA) is already working on the construction of a space platform called Planetary Transits and Oscillations of Stars (PLATO). It will carry 26 powerful telescopes and other science instruments to study the sky in more detail to look for exoplanets. Even though the Kepler Telescope and other missions have identified thousands of exoplanets, PLATO will be able to correctly assess the size, mass and age of the exoplanets it discovers. It is estimated that PLATO will be launched in 2026.

NASA's ATLAST (Advanced Technology Large Aperture Space Telescope) is another attempt to change how we view the universe. The telescope is proposed to be launched between 2025 and 2035. It will have a sensitivity about 2000 times better than the Hubble Telescope and will be able to detect even dim objects in the night sky. We have already started discovering terrestrial exoplanets similar to Earth, but ATLAST will be able to study the levels of oxygen, ozone, water and methane in such planets and identify those planets in which life forms could more easily exist.

NASA's ATLAST will have resolution much higher than the Hubble Telescope

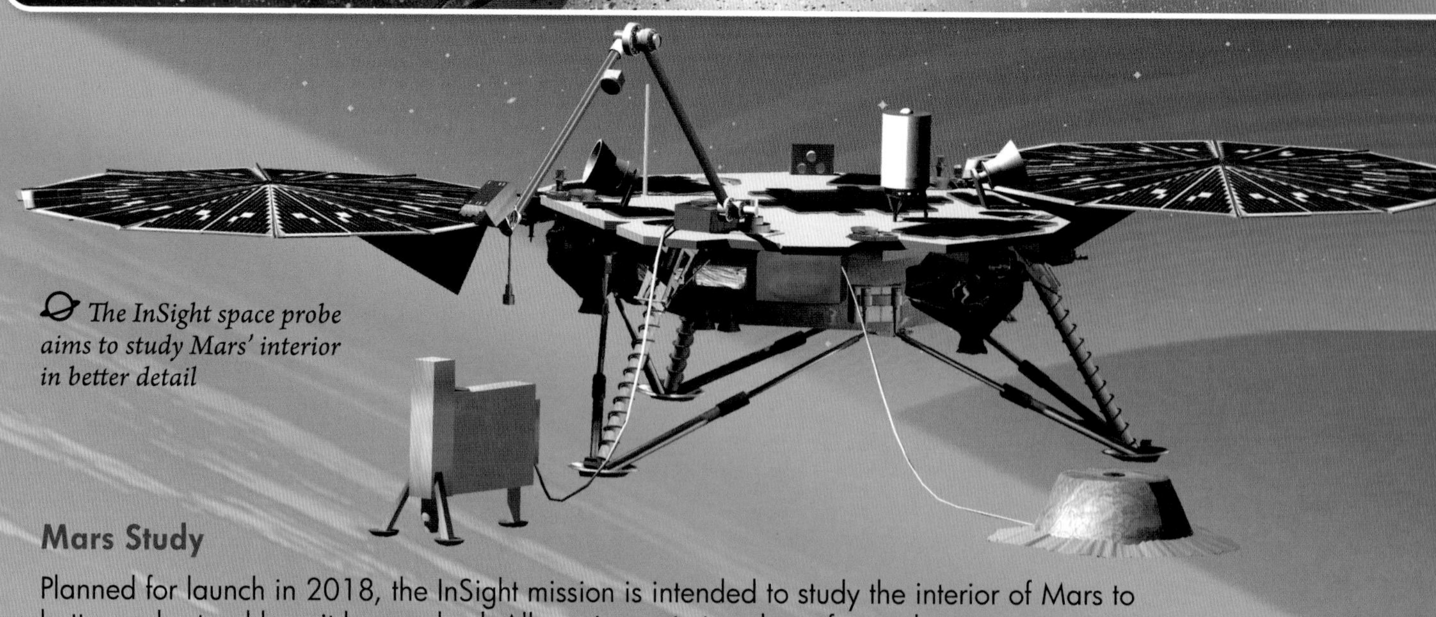

The InSight space probe aims to study Mars' interior in better detail

Mars Study

Planned for launch in 2018, the InSight mission is intended to study the interior of Mars to better understand how it has evolved. All previous missions have focused on investigating geological features on the surface such as volcanoes, craters and canyons. This lander will dig deeper into the planet than any other spacecraft has ever before.

Mars 2020 Rover will land on the red planet in 2021 and play an important role in NASA's mission to search for life on Mars. The rover will achieve this goal by looking for signs of tiny microbes or any proof that they once existed in the past. The rover will also collect rock and soil samples for research purpose. This is an important step to help prepare for human exploration and possible settlement in the near future.

Mars Settlement – A Dream Closer to Reality

A few years ago, not many would have seriously considered the possibility of humans living anywhere else in the Solar System. Now, government and private space organizations are doing research on the possibility of landing humans on Mars and possibly even establishing a permanent settlement there.

NASA is planning a mission to send astronauts to Mars sometime in the 2030s. The mission will occur in phases. The first phase of the mission will happen on the International Space Station (ISS). Here, important research on the long term impact on human health and endurance will be tested. In the next phase, astronauts will live in a deep space environment although the crew will be able to return to Earth in just a matter of days. The crew might orbit around the moon to test the capabilities of living and working at a longer distance away from Earth. The success of these phases would then enable a phase with crew spending time in low orbit around Mars or even on one of its moons before finally landing on the Martian surface. At every stage, it is hoped there might be a collaboration with other space agencies across the world, towards achieving a new milestone in the history of human exploration.

A Mars settlement might one day become a reality if conditions are favourable

While NASA is gearing up for a possible Mars landing in the 2030s, there are other space organizations like SpaceX that are planning to settle humans on Mars earlier than even what NASA has proposed. The initial goals of SpaceX would be to identify potential water sources as well as find out if there are any dangers that could prevent habitation. The preparatory phases are expected to pave the way for setting up a Martian base, that will slowly expand into a colony and eventually a thriving population on Mars capable of existing without dependence on Earth.

BepiColombo will provide better details about the smallest planet in our Solar System

Fact File

One of the biggest challenges for humans settling on Mars will be the effect of harmful radiation without a protective atmosphere.

Mercury Up Close

The ESA's mission to Mercury called BepiColombo will arrive at the planet in 2024 and orbit it in order to study the planet's various surface features. It will also try to understand how Mercury originated so close to the Sun and how it has evolved over millions of years.

Uranus and Neptune Revisit

In the next decade, NASA has plans to send missions to Uranus and Neptune. Both the planets have been visited by only one spacecraft so far – Voyager 2. It visited Uranus in 1986 and Neptune in 1989. Even with the data provided from Voyager 2 and the many observations by telescopes, the two planets are still not well understood. For instance, we still do not know the elements that make up the interior of these planets. NASA has planned for three missions to Uranus and one to Neptune in the coming years, of which at least one is to be finalised and launched in the next 20 to 25 years.

The next few decades will be an interesting time to watch out for and witness remarkable discoveries and feats in planetary exploration.

NASA has plans to send space probes to Uranus and Neptune

FACTS ABOUT PLANETS

Smallest Planet
Mercury

Hottest Planet
Venus

Only planet to host complex life
Earth

Planet with tallest mountain (Olympus Mons)
Mars

Largest Planet
Jupiter

Least Dense Planet
Saturn

Coldest Planet
Uranus

Planet farthest from the Sun
Neptune

One Complete Revolution

The time taken by a planet to circle around the Sun in its orbit once is called a revolution.

Mercury	88 Earth days
Venus	225 Earth days
Earth	365.24 days (1 Year)
Mars	1.9 Earth years
Jupiter	11.9 Earth years
Saturn	29.5 Earth years
Uranus	84 Earth years
Neptune	164.8 Earth years

Length of One Day

A 'day' is measured as the time taken by a planet to complete one rotation around itself.

Mercury	58.6 Earth days
Venus	241 Earth days
Earth	24 hours (1 day)
Mars	25 hours
Jupiter	10 hours
Saturn	11 hours
Uranus	17 hours
Neptune	16 hours

Average Temperature of Planets

The average surface temperature of planets decreases with increase in distance from the Sun. It must be noted that even though Neptune has the coldest average temperature, Uranus experiences lower temperatures (-224°C) than Neptune.

Planet	Temperature
Mercury	167°C
Venus	464°C
Earth	15°C
Mars	-65°C
Jupiter	-110°C
Saturn	-140°C
Uranus	-195°C
Neptune	-200°C

Neptune

Moons of Planets

Terrestrial planets have few or no moons, whereas the gas and ice giants have many moons. The stronger gravitational pull of the four giant planets captures more moons into their orbit than the smaller terrestrial planets.

Planet	Moons
Mercury	0
Venus	0
Earth	1
Mars	2
Jupiter	69
Saturn	62
Uranus	27
Neptune	14

Moon

Dwarf Planets

Scientists have estimated the presence of at least 200 dwarf planets in Kuiper Belt region alone. Among the dwarf planets, the most well-known are: Pluto, Ceres, Eris, Haumea and Makemake.

Dwarf Planet	Year of Discovery	One Complete Revolution	Moons
Ceres	1801	4.6 years	0
Pluto	1930	247.9 years	5
Eris	2003	561.4 years	1
Haumea	2003	281.9 years	2
Makemake	2005	305.3 years	1